The Sense of Touch

ELAINE LANDAU

Children's Press®
An Imprint of Scholastic Inc.
New York   Toronto   London   Auckland   Sydney
Mexico City   New Delhi   Hong Kong
Danbury, Connecticut

Content Consultant

Lawrence J. Cheskin, M.D.
Johns Hopkins Bloomberg School of Public Health
Baltimore, MD

Library of Congress Cataloging-in-Publication Data

Landau, Elaine.
 The sense of touch / by Elaine Landau.
    p. cm. -- (A true book)
 Includes index.
      ISBN-13: 978-0-531-16874-5 (lib. bdg.)
               978-0-531-21836-5 (pbk.)
      ISBN-10: 0-531-16874-3 (lib. bdg.)
               0-531-21836-8 (pbk.)

1. Touch--Juvenile literature. I. Title.

 QP451.L36 2008
 612.8'8--dc22   2007048082

Produced by Weldon Owen Education Inc.

1 2 3 4 5 6 7 8 9 10 R 18 17 16 15 14 13 12 11 10 09

Find the Truth!

Everything you are about to read is true *except* for one of the sentences on this page.

Which one is **TRUE**?

T or F   In order to thrive, babies need to be touched as much as they need food.

T or F   Skin makes up about 30 percent of a person's body weight.

Find the answers in this book.

3

Contents

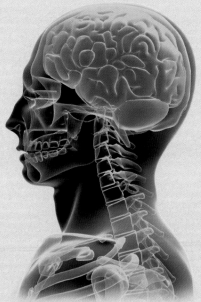

THE **BIG** TRUTH!

Amazing Arm

Your hands have thousands of touch sensors.

Your sense of touch can give you comfort. Smooth upholstery on the sofa feels better than scratchy fabric. Your cat's soft fur invites you to stroke it.

CHAPTER 1

Feeling Your Way

You're at home on a stormy night. Suddenly, there's a flash of lightning and a crack of thunder. The lights go out. Without electricity, it is pitch black in the house. "I might as well go to bed," you think. You don't bother to look for a flashlight. Instead, you decide to rely on your sense of touch to find your way.

The sense of touch is the only sense experienced all over the body.

Guided by Touch

You make slow progress. You touch walls and furniture to figure out where you are. Your feet feel the cold tiles of the kitchen floor. Ouch! You bump your toe on the kitchen table. You find the stair railing and go up. You feel for each step as you go. Finally, you feel the handle of your bedroom door. Soon you're in your cozy bed. Without your sense of touch, you would not have found your room safely.

Like your other senses, your sense of touch gives you information about your surroundings. Touch includes your skin's ability to feel pain, pressure, heat, and cold. Without it, you would never feel a brisk wind, a splash of water, or the tickle of a feather. You'd also miss the itch of a mosquito bite! Touch is important to your safety too. It lets you know if bath water is too hot or if you need to bundle up on a cold winter day.

Hands On

The **Tactile** Dome at the Exploratorium in San Francisco, California, is a three-dimensional **labyrinth**. Visitors must find their way through it in complete darkness. There is a series of chambers with different surface features and textures. You must crawl, squeeze, or slide through some of the chambers. Your sense of touch is your main guide through the Tactile Dome. However, because you cannot see, you are likely to become more aware of sounds and smells as well.

On a hot day, you may produce as many as three gallons (11 liters) of sweat.

CHAPTER 2

Getting the Message

What is the largest organ in the body? It's the skin you're in! You may not think of your skin as an organ, like your heart or lungs. Yet it is the organ that covers your entire body. It provides you with the main surface for the sensation of touch. Your skin also regulates the temperature of your body.

Skin makes up about 10 percent of a person's body weight.

All the skin cells in your epidermis are replaced with new ones about every month or so.

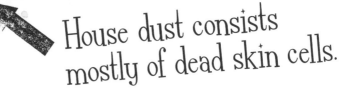

House dust consists mostly of dead skin cells.

Inside Skin

The skin has three layers, each with its own function. The **epidermis** (ep-i-DUR-mis) is the thick, tough, outer layer. It blocks germs from getting into our bodies. On its surface are dead skin cells that you continually shed. The epidermis is always making new cells to replace them.

Next is the strong, flexible **dermis**, the thickest layer of skin. This is where your **touch receptors** are. These are different kinds of nerve cells that help you feel pressure, heat, cold, and pain.

Even the skin on your eyelids has three layers. But the layers are very thin!

The innermost layer of skin is the subcutaneous (sub-kyoo-TAY-nee-uhs) tissue. It contains fat, large blood vessels, and large nerves. This layer insulates you from heat and cold. It also provides protective padding.

Human Skin

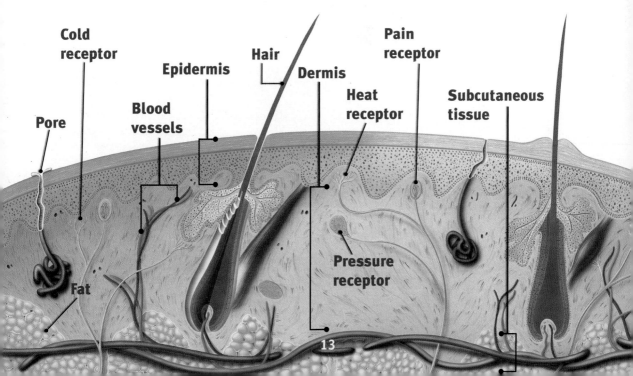

Cold receptor

Epidermis

Hair

Pain receptor

Blood vessels

Dermis

Heat receptor

Subcutaneous tissue

Pore

Fat

Pressure receptor

Where the Brain Feels

When you touch something, touch receptors in the dermis send messages to nerve cells in your **spinal cord**. The messages travel from the spinal cord to the brain's **thalamus.** The thalamus is in the middle of the brain. It is where sense messages are processed and relayed to the somatosensory (suh-mat-uh-SEN-suh-ree) cortex—the brain's touch center.

The thalamus (pink) actually lies deep in the middle of the brain, behind the lobe indicated here.

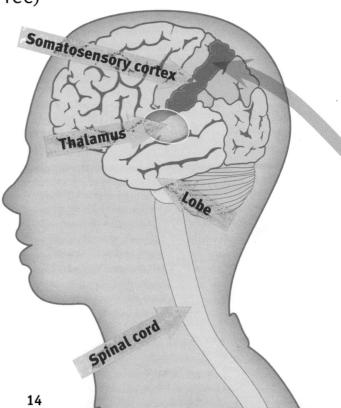

Somatosensory cortex

Thalamus

Lobe

Spinal cord

Each area of touch on your body is mapped to a special section in the somatosensory cortex. These different areas let you know where and how you are being touched. The more touch receptors a body part has, the bigger its area in the somatosensory cortex. For example, although your fingers are much smaller than your leg, a much larger area of the somatosensory cortex relates to the fingers than to the leg.

Sharing the Touch Center

Fingers

Leg

Upper lip

Somatosensory cortex

The blue bands show how much of the somatosensory cortex is devoted to some parts of the body. The area devoted to one leg is about the same as the area for one finger. The area for the upper lip is about as big as the area for three fingers.

Super Sensitive

Some parts of your body are extremely sensitive to touch. These are the parts that, like the fingers, contain lots of touch receptors and also take up a big "message" area on the somatosensory cortex. In addition to the fingers, these parts include your face, your lips and tongue, the back of your neck, and the soles of your feet.

The lips have far more cold receptors than the fingers do.

The tongue is one of the most sensitive parts of the body. The middle of the back is one of the least sensitive.

16

The sense of touch in your hands and feet is particularly important for helping you move your body safely.

Why are these body parts more sensitive than your legs? Your hands are in continual contact with your surroundings. You depend on the soles of your feet to find solid, safe ground. You eat and drink with your mouth. So you need to get as much information as possible from each of these body parts. Your legs, on the other hand, act mostly as "doers." Rather than test out your surroundings, they mainly support you. They take you places and help you do physical work. They can afford to be less "touchy" than other parts!

If the touch center of your brain was not working properly, you might have problems with your sense of balance.

18

A Feel for Your Body

Do you ever wonder how you know that you are slouching, smiling, or sitting on an unstable chair? The sense of touch is actually a family of sensations. Together, they are called the somatic sense. This includes your sense of your body's position, posture, and facial expressions. It also includes your sense of general well-being.

It is your somatic sense that "tells" you when you have a stomachache or a sudden itch for no reason. It helps you grasp a cup without dropping it. It helps you push the "on" button with just the right amount of pressure. The somatic sense includes all that we think of as touch. It also includes our general awareness of our physical selves. We depend upon this awareness. Yet we may rarely think about it.

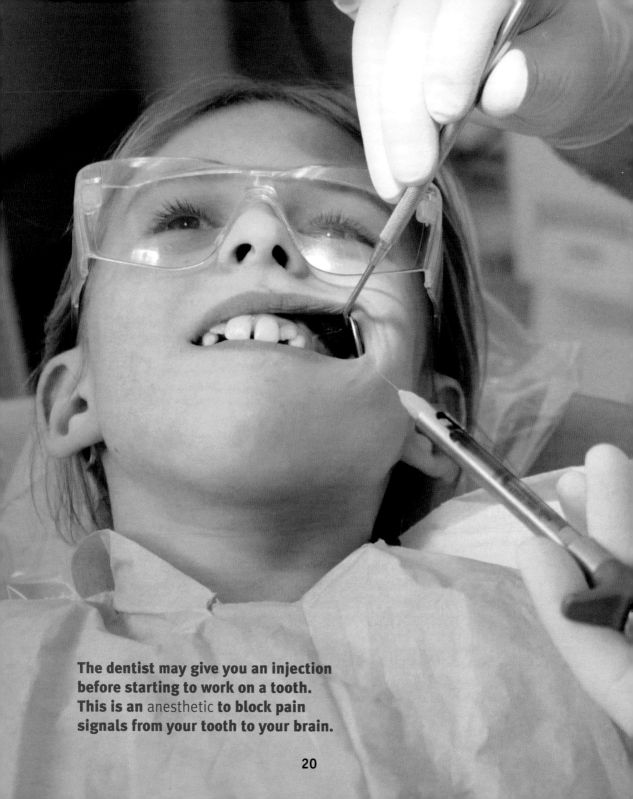

The dentist may give you an injection
before starting to work on a tooth.
This is an anesthetic to block pain
signals from your tooth to your brain.

CHAPTER 3

Out of Touch

Can you imagine losing your sense of touch? This can happen to people due to an injury or illness. The skin's touch receptors, the spinal cord, or the brain can become damaged. When this happens, the "touch" message may not get to the brain. Sometimes, the wrong message gets sent.

 Anesthetics block sensation in patients so that doctors can more easily perform operations.

Gain From Pain

Nobody likes pain. Yet feeling pain protects us. What if you broke your arm and felt no pain? You might go on using your arm and worsen the injury. Pain acts as the body's alarm system. It alerts us when something is wrong.

Some people are born unable to feel pain. They are at constant risk of injury and infection. They may not know that there is broken glass underfoot, for example. After cutting themselves, they may not know that they have an open wound. Pain is a partner in helping us stay safe.

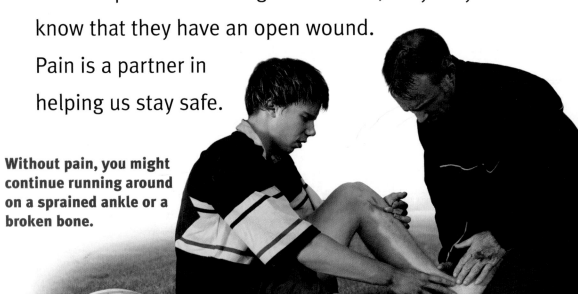

Without pain, you might continue running around on a sprained ankle or a broken bone.

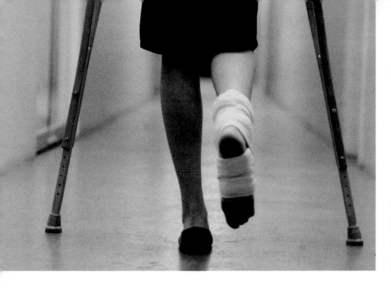

Loss of sensation in the feet is dangerous. An infection in the sole of the foot can become very serious if left untreated.

Wrong Messages

A person may feel tingling or lose all sensation as a result of injury to the brain or spinal cord. Nerves may be damaged, or nerve signals may get confused along their pathways. Similar "faulty wiring" can cause some people to feel more pain than others. Sometimes they feel pain that seems to have no cause.

Some people lose pain sensation as a result of diseases, such as diabetes. These people must be very careful where they move and walk.

Missing Messages

People who have lost one sense often rely more heavily on their other senses. People who are visually impaired rely on touch and sound. This information may actually be processed in the sight centers of their brains, as well as in the touch and sound centers. People who are hearing impaired are often unusually aware of vibrations. For this reason, they may be able to "feel" the sound of music.

Musician Evelyn Glennie is deaf. She says that deafness doesn't mean that you cannot hear. It only means there is something wrong with your ears.

Mixed Messages

Many people who have lost an arm or a leg sometimes feel as if the limb is still there and is able to move. This is called "phantom limb." New research suggests that this may be due to "cross-wiring." When a lost limb stops sending touch messages to a certain part of the brain, areas near that part of the brain may take over. The area of the brain that senses touch to the face, for example, may interpret the sensation as if it had come from the lost limb.

American surfer Bethany Hamilton experienced phantom limb pain after she lost her left arm in a shark attack.

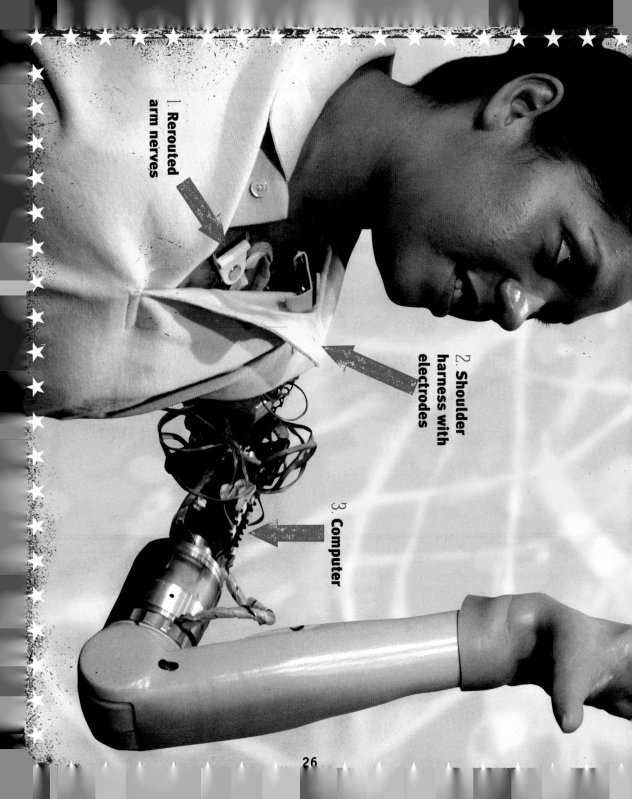

1. Rerouted arm nerves

2. Shoulder harness with electrodes

3. Computer

Amazing Arm

Claudia Mitchell lost her left arm in an accident. In 2006, she became the first woman to get a "bionic arm." Doctors rerouted the ends of the nerves on the stump of her arm to a patch of skin on her chest. Messages from her brain are passed on from here to the bionic arm. Scientists are now working on getting messages from the bionic arm to the brain. This would give the bionic arm a sense of touch!

Brain Power

Nerve impulses from the brain travel to the rerouted arm nerves on the chest. (1)

Pass It On

Messages are sent from these nerves to the electrodes on the shoulder harness. The electrodes convert the nerve impulses into electrical impulses. (2)

Command Center

The computer in the bionic arm converts the electrical impulses into commands for movement. (3)

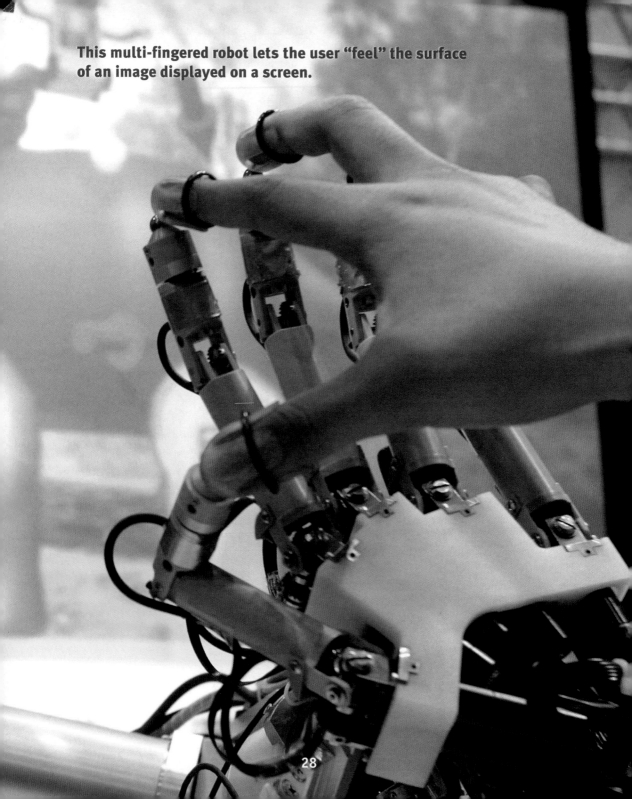

This multi-fingered robot lets the user "feel" the surface of an image displayed on a screen.

CHAPTER 4

Technology and Touch

Researchers and inventors have come up with clever ways to take advantage of our remarkable sense of touch. Some, such as the bionic arm, have medical applications. Others are simply for entertainment. All of them depend on the body's amazing sensory nervous system.

Some robot technology allows doctors to perform surgery on patients in distant cities!

Fingertips can "remember" slight variations in surface texture. That's how people learn Braille.

Reading With Touch

Braille is a reading method that relies on the sense of touch. It uses combinations of raised dots on paper to stand for letters, numbers, and symbols. Braille readers feel the dots with their fingers.

Before the invention of Braille, people who were blind had no way to read books on their own. Now, more than 600,000 books and magazines are printed in Braille every year. Even the Harry Potter books are published in Braille!

Fixing With Touch

Amazing touch technology is giving people who are visually impaired a way to look at things. One invention uses a tiny video camera to film a person's surroundings. The input from the camera is converted by a computer into coded electrical impulses. These are passed to a small metal pad on the person's tongue. At first, the person feels only a tingling sensation on the tongue. However, with practice, the code begins to make sense. The brain learns to translate the code into a visual image!

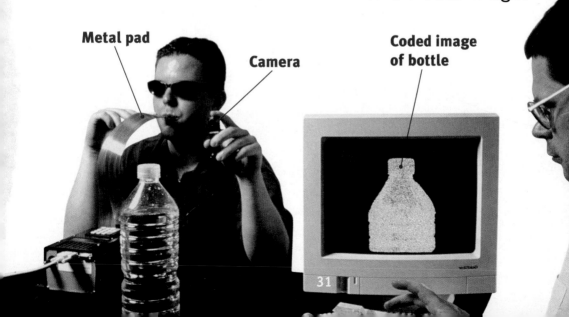

Metal pad

Camera

Coded image of bottle

Transatlantic Touch

Transatlantic touch is a long-distance online group experience. A small robotic arm takes the place of a computer mouse. Users at several computers see a three-dimensional room on their screens. They also see an object and their own "locations" within the room. Together, the users "feel" and "lift" the onscreen object. The robotic arm allows the users to sense the object's weight and shape. They are also able to sense the actions of the other users.

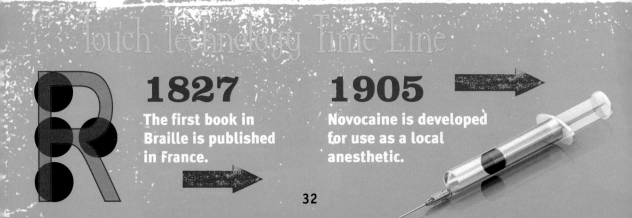

Touch Technology Time Line

1827
The first book in Braille is published in France.

1905
Novocaine is developed for use as a local anesthetic.

This robotic arm works like a computer mouse.

Web sites may soon include a touch feature. An adaptation in the user's mouse will make this work. Imagine feeling a surfboard slam against a huge wave, without ever leaving your chair. The phrase "surfing the Web" would take on a whole new meaning! Adding touch will also help shoppers. See a sweater you want to buy online? One day, you may be able to know before you buy it whether it feels soft or scratchy!

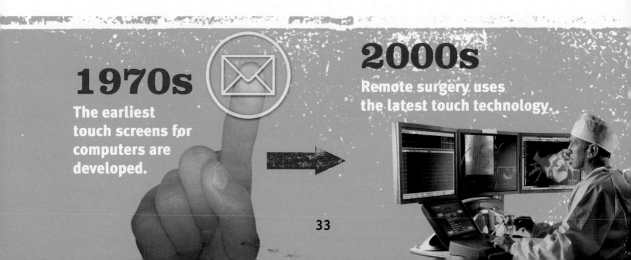

1970s
The earliest touch screens for computers are developed.

2000s
Remote surgery uses the latest touch technology.

CHAPTER 5

We Need Touch So Much!

What do babies need as much as food in order to survive? The answer is touch! Touch is one of the first ways parents connect to their children. Studies have shown that infants can live without sight, smell, or hearing. Yet they must be touched to survive.

 Babies who are rarely touched have smaller brains than those who are cuddled a lot.

Even in the 1950s, touching newborns was not encouraged as much as it is today.

The Magic Touch

The need for touch may seem like common sense. However, in the early 1900s, people in Europe and North America believed that touching newborns was not good for them. They thought that it would spread germs and make the babies weak and whiny. In European orphanages at that time, it was not permitted to cuddle newborn babies. Although the babies were well fed and cared for, many of them became ill. Some even died. Then one doctor insisted that the babies be held several times daily. The sick babies immediately began to thrive.

Recent research has confirmed the importance of touch for babies. In a 1986 study, 40 **premature** infants were briefly massaged three times a day. A second group was not massaged. The massaged infants put on more weight and were more active and alert.

Today, parents and nurses are encouraged to touch and stroke premature babies as much as possible.

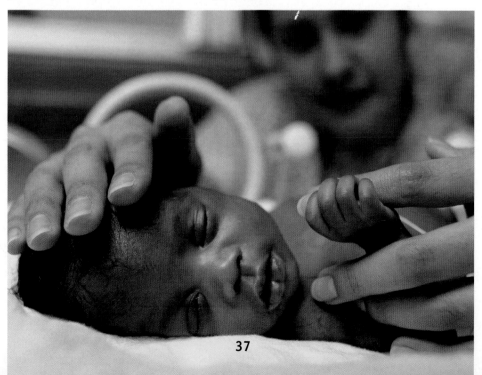

Hugs and Handshakes

Long after infancy, touch continues to be important. Touch is the simplest language of communication. Many societies have some kind of customary greeting that involves a hug, a handshake, or a kiss on the cheek. A pat on the back is one way to show approval. A squeeze of the hand can communicate sympathy or affection.

Touch can also play a role in doing good work. Today, some businesses offer their employees **massage therapy** breaks during the workday. The workers are more relaxed and do a better job.

Various peoples, such as the Maori of New Zealand, touch noses as a form of greeting.

Maori use this form of greeting for family and friends, as well as for heads of state.

Animals Touch Too

Many animal species use touch as a form of communicating and bonding. Like humans, many mammals are comforted by physical contact. Horses often rub their necks against each other. Elephants lean together and intertwine their trunks. Kittens and puppies cuddle together to sleep. It seems that animals, like humans, benefit from being touched.

Mammal mothers, such as giraffes, nuzzle and lick their young.

Dogs have touch receptors in their whiskers. ➡

Pet Your Pet

Touch is important for good health. Petting an animal has been shown to have a calming effect on people. Studies reveal that it even acts to lower high blood pressure. Patients often recover more quickly if they regularly pet an animal. For that reason, therapy dogs are sometimes brought to visit people in hospitals and nursing homes. Their soothing presence is good medicine!

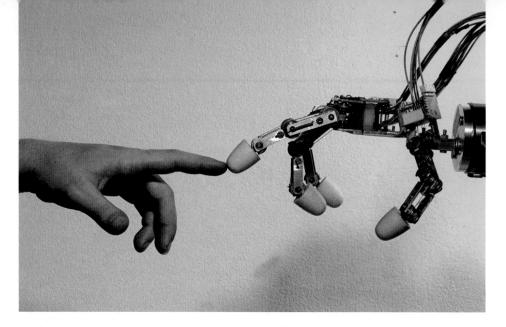

Someday soon, scientists hope that artificial limbs will actually be able to "feel" when somebody touches them!

Touch and the Future

Our sense of touch is involved in all aspects of our lives. Because it happens in every part of the body, it constantly gives us information about everything we are doing. Scientists are still making discoveries about this complicated sense and improving touch-based technologies. No doubt, these technologies will expand our experience of the world. ★

True Statistics

First sense to develop in a human being:
Touch

Last sense to be lost in old age: Touch

Number of age receptors left at age 70:
50 percent

Numbers of various touch receptors:
For every 200 pain receptors in a person's skin, there are about 15 pressure receptors, 6 cold receptors, and 1 heat receptor

Total length of nerves in the skin:
About 45 miles (72 kilometers)

Speed of touch signals:
Up to 200 feet (61 meters) per second

Did you find the truth?

(T) In order to thrive, babies need to be touched as much as they need food.

(F) Skin makes up about 30 percent of a person's body weight.

Resources

Books

Collins, Andrew. *See, Hear, Smell, Taste, and Touch: Using Your Five Senses* (National Geographic Science Chapters). Des Moines, IA: National Geographic, 2006.

Ganeri, Anita. *Your Senses*. Milwaukee, WI: Gareth Stevens, 2003.

Pringle, Laurence. *Touch* (Explore Your Senses). Tarrytown, NY: Benchmark Books, 2000.

Romanek, Trudee. *Wow! The Most Interesting Book You'll Ever Read About the Five Senses*. Toronto, Kids Can Press, 2004.

Seuling, Barbara. *Your Skin Weighs More Than Your Brain: and Other Freaky Facts About Your Skin, Skeleton, and Other Body Parts*. Mankato, MN: Picture Window Books, 2008.

Stewart, Melissa. *Use Your Senses*. Mankato, MN: Compass Point Books, 2005.

Tatham, Betty. *How Animals Shed Their Skin*. Danbury, CT: Franklin Watts, 2002.

Taylor-Butler, Christine. *The Nervous System* (A True Book: Health and the Human Body). Danbury, CT: Children's Press, 2008.

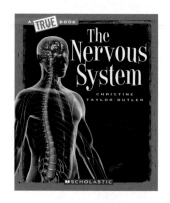

Organizations and Web Sites

ThinkQuest

http://library.thinkquest.org/3750/touch/touch.html
Read some interesting facts about the sense of touch,
and learn more about Braille.

Neuroscience for Kids

http://faculty.washington.edu/chudler/chtouch.html
Test your sense of touch with some of these fun experiments.

Sun Safety for Kids

www.sunsafetyforkids.org
Don't miss this Web site for some great information
on protecting your skin from the sun's harmful rays.

Places to Visit

The Exploratorium: Museum of Science, Art, and Human Perception

Palace of Fine Arts
3601 Lyon Street
San Francisco, CA 94123
(415) 561 0399
www.exploratorium.edu
Discover your sense of touch
in the amazing Tactile Dome
—where no one says
"Don't touch!"

MIT Museum

265 Massachusetts Avenue
N52-200
Cambridge, MA 02139
(617) 253 9607
http://web.mit.edu/museum/
See the Robots and Beyond
exhibition to find out more
about the technology of
"virtual touch."

Important Words

anesthetic (an-iss-THET-ik) – a drug given to people to prevent them from feeling pain

Braille (BRAYL) – a system of writing and printing for people who are visually impaired

dermis – the flexible, middle layer of skin

epidermis – the thick, tough, outer layer of skin

labyrinth (LAB-uh-rinth) – complicated system of paths or tunnels through which it is difficult to find one's way

massage therapy – professional treatment involving kneading the muscles to relieve stress or health problems

premature (pree-muh-CHOOR) – happening before the usual or expected time

spinal cord – a thick cord of nerve tissue that runs through the spinal column. It connects the brain to the rest of the nerves in the body.

tactile (TAK-tyle) – of, or relating to, the sense of touch

thalamus – an area in the middle of the brain that processes information from the senses and passes it on to other parts of the brain

touch receptors – different kinds of nerve cells that sense pressure, heat, cold, and pain

Index

Page numbers in **bold** indicate illustrations.

About the Author

Award-winning author Elaine Landau has a bachelor's degree from New York University and a master's degree in library and information science. She has written more than 300 nonfiction books for children and young adults.

Ms. Landau strongly relies on her sense of touch when sculpting clay figures with her son. It's a hobby they both enjoy. She lives in Miami, Florida, with her husband and son. You can visit her at her Web site: www.elainelandau.com.

PHOTOGRAPHS: Big Stock Photo (© Jose Manuel Gelpi Diaz, p. 16; p. 30; p. 32; hand, p. 33); Digital Vision (p. 40); © Exploratorium/www.exploratorium.edu (p. 9); Getty Images (p. 22; p. 25; p. 28; p. 37); © Hansen Medical (remote surgery, p. 33); iStockphoto.com (© Anne Marie Kurtz, p. 34; © Elena Elisseeva, p.18; © Julian Rovagnati, p. 10; © Nicole S. Young, p. 5; © Sebastian Kaulitzki, p. 4; © Shawn Gearhart, p. 3 ; © Webphotographeer, handshake, p. 5; © Valerie Loiseleux, p. 17; p. 43); © Jamshed Mistry (front cover); Photolibrary (p. 12; p. 20; p. 31; pp. 41–42); PhotoNewZealand (p. 39); PHANTOM Omni ® haptic device, manufactured by SensAble Technologies, Inc.® (top, p. 33); Stockxpert (Eric Isselée, back cover); Tranz (Corbis, p. 6; p. 23; p. 36; Reuters, p. 26; Rex Features, p. 24)